HOW TO DEAL RUTHLESSLY WITH CONSPIRACY

BY BISHOP INNOCENT

I was shocked by these three stories.

First is the story of John Jameson.
He worked as an editor with an African magazine. Before he came on board, the newspaper was making a loss.
Everything the managers did deepened the nosedive. For five years the business was in the woods.

However the arrival of John marked a reversal. Things began to pick up. It was as if someone had poured some sugar on the floor. Like ants, people began to hover around the brand and to make it a magazine of their choice. Within three months, the accounts came out of red. By the sixth month, all debts were settled. Profit began to climb higher and higher to the joy of the media owners.

Then also began the problems of John. Without knowing that John understood the local language, local folks began to

play a game of nepotism. They
complained loud and long that
journalism, let alone editing, was not
rocket science. The fact that John could
speak and understand the local language
was however not known to the local
folks. Therefore, it was easy for them to
throw caution to the wind. One morning
three indigenous staff of the news media
came to the managing director. John
was in the same office at the time. They
brazenly demanded John's sack.

According to them they needed a citizen
whether competent or not.
They insisted that though it was
economically right to appoint the right
person for the position, it was not
politically justifiable in a Third World
country to appoint an expatriate editor.
They were ready to raise a political riot
in support of their cause.

The managing director could see that it
was a conspiracy.

The second story has to do with a young Israeli boy. I guess you are familiar with this Bible story. This beloved boy had eleven wicked brothers. One day, he and his brothers went to their father's farm. While they were on the farm, they all talked peacefully and with love to one another. Any one who saw them at that moment would cherish the love between the brothers.
However once they saw a caravan of trade passing by, the wicked brothers changed. Their hidden wickedness came out as they held a secret meeting and decided to sell their twelveth brother to the traders.
They made an offer and the international trader accepted. paid for the boy whose name was Joseph and took him into captivity.
 It was also a terrible conspiracy.

 The third story is also about a gang up. It has to do with the constantly

traveling managing director of Marks
and Spencers. The director had been
away for some time now. He was
therefore expected home at any
moment. So everyone was busy putting
the house in order so that the man
would not come and meet the business
in disarray.

The managing director relied on a hand-
picked supervisor. This evening the
supervisor worked hard with the
accounts officer to balance the account.
The supervisor knew that to whom
much is given, much is expected. The
MD had broken several protocols to pick
him from afar to supervise the business.

The supervisor believed that the only
way to compensate the MD was to work
extra hard and he indeed put his best
foot forward.
 Unknown to him, many in the office
envied him. They note only wished him
down, they plotted his downfall.

This particular evening, before the supervisor left the office, he co-signed a trial balance account. The accounts officer also appended his signature, attesting to the fact that all was well with the finances in the company.

The next morning the supervisor was shocked when the MD issued him a query. The allegation was that the account did not balance.

To enable him answer the query, the supervisor went through with a toothpick. He had to call in an outsider since he was not good in accounting and he could not trust the accounts officer since he prepared the one now being subjected to an integrity test.

After a thorough investigation, it was found that the accounts officer and the assistant supervisor planned to doctor the accounts to look as if the supervisor had issued a loan to himself, a corporate taboo that would have infuriated the managing director and possibly lead to the sacking of the supervisor.

Of course, the coup plotters got the sack instead.

These three stories keep ringing bells in my head. And make me realise that conspiracy is extreme wickedness from the pit of hell and must be dealt with as it should.

THEY SAID IT

CONSPIRACY?

A <u>secret</u> plan made by two or more people to do something that is <u>harmful</u> or <u>illegal</u> a <u>secret</u> plan made by two or more people to do something that is <u>harmful</u> or <u>illegal</u>.

-courtesy of ***Longman Dictionary of Contemporary English***

IS CONSPIRACY A NEW THING?

.

Conspiracy is not a strange thing to the Earth. There are some cases of conspiracy in the Bible.
Below are a few;
1. **Even in heaven**, there was a case of conspiracy. Lucifer and his men conspired against God. Take a look at the Bible account of it:

2. **The brothers of Joseph**, which is one of the three stories earlier mentioned above, also conspired against him. They planned initially to kill him but when they saw a caravan coming, they changed

their minds and sold him to the traders.

3. Another **Bible account in the book of Esther,** has it that two men conspired against the king. That was during the time of Mordecai the Jew in Susa and during the time of Queen Vashti.

4. Another case of conspiracy, **involved King Ahab and his wicked wife Jezebel.** They conspired against an innocent farmer and killed him. They did not stop there. They told lies against him and took over his vineyard.
The Conspiracy was due to curvaceousness.

5. **Judas Iachariot was in a conspiracy against Jesus Christ.** The high priest, the Sadducees and the Pharisees all conspired with Judas against Jesus Christ who was

subsequently arrested and taken to the Roman authorities for trial based on trumped-up charges..

6. **During the time of King Darius,** there was also a conspiracy against Daniel and all other exiles. They wanted the king to kill all the exiles because they knew that they would not bow to calved images. So they told the King to permit them to have his image carved and placed in public so that everyone could come and bow.

The king approved it and as was expected, the brave exiles did not shy away. Instead Daniel led them to pray in public in defiance of the decree.

The king did not disappoint the plotters. As expected also, he ordered that Daniel be thrown into the lion's den. It was a conspiracy by those who were jealous of Daniel and the other brilliant exiles.

7. In Numbers 22, **Prophet Balaam was also hired by King Balak of Moab in a conspiracy to curse the Israelites**. Remember that they committed no offence. They were bypassing into the Promised Land and the King of Moab tried to stop them from reaching the Promised Land.

THE CRIES OF A CONSPIRACY VICTIM

"Deal with them as with Midian,

As with Sisera,

As with Jabin at the Brook Kishon,

Who perished at En Dor,

Who became a refuse on the earth.

Make their nobles like Oreb and like Zeeb,

Yes, all their princes like Zebah and Zalmunna,

Who said, "Let us take for ourselves

The pastures of God for a possession."

O my God, make them like the whirling dust,

Like the chaff before the wind!

As the fire burns the woods,

And as the flame sets the mountains on fire,

So pursue them with Your tempest,

And frighten them with Your storm.

Fill their faces with shame,

That they may seek Your name, O Lord.

Let them be [e]confounded and dismayed forever;

Yes, let them be put to shame and perish.

That they may know that You, whose name alone is the Lord,

*Are the Most High over all the
earth."*

-   **Psalm 83; 9-18**

CHAPTER TWO

CONSEQUENCES OF CONSPIRACIES

1. **It leads to hatred**. If those being conspired against are not matured enough, the attack on them can make them hate the coup plotters. On another hand, when they spread lies against innocent people, others may be deceived into hating those under attack for no just reason.

2. **It also leads to betrayals.** Conspirators are willing to do anything to get what they want. In the process, they locate other people's weaknesses and seek to

use those in forcing them to do their bidding or be removed.

3. **People often lose confidence in the person being betrayed** or attacked. Conspirators spread lies and falsehood against their victims. Most times such fake information portray the victim as incompetent and not fit for the position presently occupied.

4. **They make the office hostile**. Those who are conspiring knowingly or unknowingly, make the office environment too harsh and hostile for the victim to dwell in, in peace.

5. **Conspiracies also erode trust**. When people paint you black and say things that are not true about you to others, as noted earlier, their hearers first lose

confidence in you and end up not trusting you as before.

6. **It leads to cheap blackmail.** If the victim is not strong-willed, he caves in to their demands and throws in the towel.

7. **It destroys team spirit**. Conspiracies put a knife that holds workers together. Thus, they can no longer be on the same page. People who have been working together in harmony begin to play each other hanky panky.

8. **Characters are defamed permanently.** Sometimes the damage is so much that even when the victim leaves the environment. The stigma still follows him or her. Most times conspirators tell lies. They also slander people you know in order to get others to work with them.

9. Conspiracies are known to **lead to suicide**.

10.   Conspiracy lures others into **sharing the sin of others.** It is a sad story of luring innocent people into sharing the sins of others. This happens when they hear falsehood and concocted accusations against others and join in without verification. Thus, they share in the sin of the original conspirators.

11. **Conspiracy turns people into monsters.** Often, conspirators behave like people who have their conscience seared with hot iron. So they do things without thinking of the consequences.people who were once known for meekness, become lionised, just to do others in.

12. **Conspiracy encourages materialism.** Most times innocent people are sucked in just for a mess of porridge.

13. **It invariably leads to rebellion.** This is often the case when the request of the plotters are not acceded to. The shame of being found to be fake or of their failure, lead conspirators into rebellion against constituted authority. If for no other reasons, just to cover their tracks. Permit me to digress and remind you that the Bible says the rebellion is worse than witchcraft.

14. **It leads to witchcraft.** In extreme cases, in order to make sure that they achieve their aim, conspirators engage in black magic and witchcraft. Victims of conspiracy, especially in high profile offices, report that on

occasions, they have entered their office only to find fetish objects dumped there either to intimidate or harm them.

15. **It ends in shame.** This unfortunately, works in two ways; on one hand, when eventually the conspiracy is discovered to be what it is, conspirators lose face and suffer shame. On the other hand, when the truth remains hidden, which is rare in the end, innocent people lose face and ot Conspiracy is the work Of wicked spirits. we must all bear this in mind and the only way to overcome wicked Wicked spirits is to raise a standard against them and that standard is the name of Jesus Christ the name that is above all names in prayers

CHAPTER THREE

REMEMBER ALWAYS

1. The conspiracy of Lucifer and his angels did not change god and God made us in his image. therefore the conspiracy of people against us should not change yours. we should remain who we are inspite and despite they're conspiracies.

2. The conspiracy of the brothers of Joseph ended in the good of all. The Bible says in Romans 8; 28 that all things work it out for the good of them that believe.

3. The Conspiracy against Jesus
    Christ, contrary to the
    expectations of the conspirators,
    only helped him to achieve or
    fulfill his ministry of redemption
    of mankind.

4. The Conspiracy against Mordecai
    and the Jews during the era of
    King Darius led to the death of
    their enemies. Those who planned
    their downfall reaped what they
    sowed.

5. The Conspiracy against Joseph by
    his brothers helped him to become
    a prime minister in a foreign
    nation.

6. We must not also forget the
    conspiracy of King Ahab and his
    wife led to their painful death. I
    repeat every conspirator shall reap
    what they sow because the Bible
    says that as long as the Earth

remaineth, seed time and harvest
time shall not cease.

7. We must all bear in mind that the
   word of God cannot be broken.
   The Lord means it when he says
   that all things work for the good of
   those who believe. It does not
   matter what the conspirator does
   or how well they conspire.

   The scripture also says that they
   shall gather but surely they must
   scatter.

   Are people conspiring against you?
   Fear not for there is no
   enchantment against Jacob. The
   sceptre of the wicked shall not rest
   on the justified and righteous in
   Christ Jesus.

CHAPTER FOUR

TAKE NOTE OF THE FOLLOWING;

1. In all three stories told at the beginning of this book, there were gang ups. We saw situations where a group of people came together to work evil.

2. Intentions in all were bad. The conspirators never planned for the well being of their victims.

3. They had evil meetings where they hatched their plans. These are normally nocturnal meetings held

without the knowledge of the intended victims.

4. Their meetings were both immoral and unlawful. Most times, the conspirators steal official work hours to hatch their plans when they should have been working for the progress of the establishment.

5. Their actions were shrouded in secrecy. Conspirators always have those they must not be privy to their plans till the deal is done.

6. All three were conspiracies aimed at harming somebody. Sometimes, conspirators work bodily harm into their plans.

7. They never gave their
    targets a chance to apologize
    for any offence. They try you
    in your absence and find you
    guilty on their own terms.

8. They did not care what the
    victim's reaction would be.
    You might as well go to hell
    for all they care.

9. They behave as people who
    have no conscience. And so
    it is to date . Those who
    conspire against others are
    wicked and act without
    conscience, planning only to
    hurt the innocent.

SO WHY NOT DISAPPOINT THEM?

Do not lapse into self-pity. It is
really not about you in person. It is in

their nature. If you were not there at the time, they would have latched on to someone else.

This time however, they have jammed rock because you are too defended by the Lord God of Hosts to be intimidated by anyone as we see in the next chapter.

CHAPTER FIVE

ARE YOU CURRENTLY IN THIS SITUATION?

1. Are some people ganging up against you and other innocent people?

2. Are they holding secret meetings against you?

3. Are they planning to harm you for no cogent reason.

4. Are they having only greed and hatred as reasons, as is often the case, for their action but go ahead all the same?

5. Are they not accusing the innocent based on trumped-up charges?

6. Do they hate you despite the fact that you love them?

7. Is their wicked goal not just to get you out of position and possibly replace you with one of their own?

8. Have they accused and tried you in absentia?

9. Are they not spreading falsehood against you? Perhaps just to give a dog a bad name in order to hang it?

10.   Are they not even accusing you of owning some fictitious debts?.

AND SO WHAT?

Did they not accuse the early apostles?
Did they not gang up against Jesus
Christ? Do the scriptures not tell us that
Jesus Christ is the same yesterday and
today? That he changes not? So why
worry?

Do not panic. Be strong. He that
watches over Israel, neither sleeps nor
slumber. You are not the first to be in
this kind of situation.

Also, do not resort to any of the
following self help actions as most non
Christians and immature Christians
would want to do.

"11 Lest Satan should get an advantage over us: for we are not ignorant of his devices."

\-   **2 Corinthians 2;11 [KJV]**

CHAPTER SIX

THINGS PEOPLE DEVOID OF UNDERSTANDING DO WHEN OTHERS CONSPIRE AGAINST THEM

These are things the devil will expect you to do. We must refuse to do them and resist the devil with the Grace of God in us.

We must not be ignorant of these things for the Bible says in **Hosea 4;6** that due to ignorance, my people perish;

The devil after inspiring his people to gang up against you, will be expecting you to:

1. Get angry. Once in such a position you can do anything including that which defames the faith in Christ Jesus that you and I profess.

2. Some victims of conspiracy are known to go into physical confrontation with the conspirators. That is akin to going into the mud with a pig!

3. Others get into arguments and trading of insults. A child of God should be meek and long suffering.

4. Other victims get very bitter. This can lead to hatred and unforgiveness. It is a hard saying but then the Bible says we should forgive our enemies and pray for them. Jesus Christ prayed for the thieves on the cross with him and forgave those who hung him on the cross. We are his disciples when we obey his instructions in full and not partially or selectively as many baby christians and unbelievers do.

5. Many victims lose their handle. Then, they turn the office into a boxing ring. A mature child of God would have to walk away no matter how difficult that would be hard to do.

6. Others allow worry to take over their life. They allow concern to raise their blood pressure. Before

you know it they become
candidates for hospitals to the joy
of those who are attacking them.

7. Some victims feel so threatened
that they resign. Never do what
the devil wants you to do. Never
recuse yourself from corporate
activities. Doing that is
tantamount to playing into the
hand of your accusers.

**SO NOTE THE ABOVE AND
TRAIN YOURSELF TO FIGHT
THE GOOD FIGHT.**

Never give up. Remember once
more that though you are
persecuted, you can never be
abandoned! God promised us to be
the Fourth Man in every fire of
life. He has done it before, he will
do it again.
Note of the above and train
yourself to resist the devil when he

ever and wherever he suggests any
of these negative reactions to you.
None of them should be the
conduct of a child of God.

Now, let us end with a summary,
in the next but short chapter,
which tells us what a mature child
of God should do under the
circumstance.

HOW TO DEAL RUTHLESSLY WITH CONSPIRACIES AS A CHILD OF GOD

As Children of God, the Bible tells us but the name of the Lord is a strong Tower. Those that run under it are protected. Anybody that names the name of the Lord is hidden in Christ Jesus and therefore unreachable.

1. Therefore, a time of conspiracy is a time to **activate your strong faith** in God. the Bible says those that know the God they serve shall be strong and do exploits. Such persons are not moved by events around them but by the word of God. Believe that God is well able to save and deliver no matter how many people gang-up or how they do it.

2. **Remain calm in the face of provocation**. Do not allow their conspiracies and machinations to rearrange you. Be yourself and keep doing the good you are known for. Do not enter into the gutter with the wicked. Remember that the Bible says all things work out for the good of those who believe. Know that these too will work in your favor. Mordecai did not take the law into

his own hands. So too should you
not take the law into your own
hands.

3. A conspiracy against you is **a call
to increased prayer.** I know
you must have been praying. This
is the time to pray more. Go into
your closet, onto your knees, and
cry unto the Lord. Pray in season
and out of season.
 Our God surely answers prayers.
Pray until the lines fall onto you
in pleasant places.

4. **Invite others to pray with you**.
The Bible says that the fervent
effectual prayer of the faithful
man, avails much. It also says if
two shall agree, it shall be
established. Get sincere Christian
brothers or brethren and agree
with them in prayer concerning
the crazy conspiracy against you

and every mountain will be made plain, in Jesus name.

5. **Fast over it.** When situations seem intractable, we add fasting to normal prayers. Jesus Christ educated us to the fact when he said; ***this type requires fasting.***

6. **Prayerfully approach your superiors and explain** things from your own perspective. Mordecai at his own time, encouraged Esther to approach the King with a petition and that made the difference. a

7. **Relax.** Allow God to fight for you. Worrying only adds lines to your wrinkles and increases your blood pressure. Remember that if you break down your enemies will be highly elated. Therefore take the

matter to the Lord and leave it there.

8. Know however, that it is not enough to pray; **you must pray with the word of God.** The Lord gave his word for this purpose.
The Devil knows the word of the Lord and when you put it to him, it is like showing the drunk-and-drive man what the law says about driving after drinking. He is then left with no option than to comply. As you read further, you will find 40 prayer points at the end of this book to guide you.

9. **Pick your battles!** Never allow the fact that a few persons are conspiring against you, to make you see everyone in and around you as an enemy. Better it is, to see everybody as a friend than to see everyone as an enemy.

10.   **Be kind enough to pray for the repentance of the enemy.** Renew your mind always with the word of God. By so doing, you will not fall into bitterness and the consequences of bitterness.

11. **Be extra vigilant**. A time of gang-ups, is a time to watch and pray. [**Math 26;41**].

12. **Be cheerful.** Never award your enemies the pleasure of seeing you frustrated.
You will not be frustrated, in Jesus name.

13. Permit me to repeat; it is very **important that you renew your mind always.** At a time like this, the devil and his agents, assisted by your flesh, will be working hard to remind you of the presumed gravity of what offence

and punishment await you, should
you be found guilty of what they
accuse you of.
Just ignore them and move on
with your life.

14. **Above all fear not!** Be bold and
courageous. Meditate upon the
word of the Lord day in day out.
Then you shall have good success
and victory over you are enemies.
[Joshua 1:1-8]
You shall not see shame!
Wherever they have plotted your
downfall, you shall see them with
your own eyes as they hang in
their own Gallows unless they
repent!
**Put your trust absolutely in
the Lord.** Do your part by
praying; then leave the rest to
God. Victory is certain for those
who put their trust in the Lord.

Do not forget to pray constantly and be guided by the 40 prayer points below.

Thank you and stay blessed.

FORTY PRAYER POINTS AGAINST CONSPIRACIES AND CONSPIRATORS

1. Father in heaven, **I thank you** for making me see this day. May your name be praised forever.

2. **Forgive me** my sins, oh Lord and wash me clean with the precious Blood of Jesus Christ.

3. It is written that at the mention of Jesus Christ every knee shall bow. In the name of Jesus Christ, **I bind the devil and his agents**

and kick them out of these
prayers.

4. It is written that they shall gather
   but **they shall surely scatter.**
   Lord, please scatter as many as
   have gathered against me.

5. It is written that **a man reaps
   what he sows.** Lord, let all
   conspirators reap the fruits of
   their labour. I pray in Jesus' name.

6. When Nebuchadnezzar saw that
   Daniel was not harmed in the
   lion's den, he acknowledged your
   supremacy; Father, give my
   enemies reasons to acknowledge
   you. I pray in Jesus' name.

7. Father, **open the eyes of my
   superiors** to see that my accusers
   are liars and blackmail is. Lord
   expose their deceit and duplicity.

8. It is written Lord, that **there is no enchantment against Jacob.** Lord there shall be no enchantment against me.

9. It is written that **in vain do the nations rage.** Let all conspirators rage in vain, oh Lord.

10.   Just as how Harmmon built a gallow for Mordecai, but hung on it, **may my accusers hang on their own gallow**s.

11. Oh Lord my God my, **help me to jump over every pit** they dig. I pray in Jesus' name.

12. **Let the counsel of the wicked not stand;** for who can say no when you say yes?

13. Oh Lord, **do not allow my enemies to triumph** over me,

for I put my trust in you absolutely.

14. Oh Lord, make my accusers repent and **retrace their steps** before it is too late.

15. If they fail to repent, Lord **cast them out** the way Lucifer was irretrievably cast out of heaven.

16. Lord, put a spook amongst them, so **that they no more speak with one voice.**

17. **Expose their lies** oh Lord! Put them to shame. I pray in Jesus' name.

18. I put my trust in you Lord. Therefore, **put them to shame,** no matter how they gather and no matter how they conspire.

19. **I decree confusion in their midst.** They shall fight one another from today onwards.

20. It is written that whatsoever I decree on earth is decreed in heaven. Therefore **I decree victory for me over evil**. I pray in Jesus' name.

21. **I decree all ears blocked against their lies** and falsehood as well as against their false Witnesses.

22. **Make them fall** out of favour like Harman.

23. **May they be removed** from my environment as Harmon was removed from office in the Bible book of Esther.

24.   **Make them bow to thy Glory;** as Joseph's brothers bowed to him in the end.

25.   Mayday **eat their own vomit**. Like dogs without shame.

26.   May whatever they depend on **disappoint them** as they conspire against me.

27.   Oh Lord, **turn their curses against me into blessings**. I pray in Jesus' name.

28.   Oh Lord, **send a donkey to speak to them** as you sent against Balaam and King Balak of Moab. I pray in Jesus' name.

29.   **Let every of their plans, turn-out in my favor;** For your word says that all things work out for the good of those who believe.

30.   **Lord keep me** the way you kept Daniel in the Lion's den.

31. Anywhere the conspirators are taking my name to, **let them be rejected.**

32.   **Any altar they raise against me, let it be shattered to pieces** and silenced with the precious Blood of Jesus.

33.   **Any spiritual prison prepared for me, let my enemies go inside** and stay. I pray in Jesus' name.

34.   **I break every chain;** physical and spiritual put on my leg by conspiracies in Jesus name.

35.   **Lord, cause them to repent or perish.** Spare not the wicked so that they will not rejoice in their wickedness.

36.	**Oh God, manifest your power** in my life so that my enemies may see your goodness I pray in Jesus name.

37.	Like Judas Iscariot, let every conspirator who refuses to repent, **kill themselves with their own hands** I decree in Jesus.

38.	**Oh Lord, arise** and let it not be said that you are not able to save those who look up to you.

39.	Oh Lord, **let not the wicked say; where is my God?**

40.	**Thank you Father for I know that you hear me always.** This hour will not be an exception. I pray in Jesus' name.

HELP US TO HELP OTHERS

If you enjoyed this book, please help us proceed to Amazon and write a review.

It can guide a person who deserves your guidance in choosing a helpful book.

Your sincere view will also help us to edit this book for better comprehension and to add or minus where needs be.

Thanks in anticipation.

-Bishop Ochei Innocent.

OTHER BOOKS BY SAME AUTHOR

1. ACIDIC PRAYERS TO BREAK BAD HABITS.

2. DANGERS OF ORDINATION - AND WHY WHO ORDAINS YOU IS VERY IMPORTANT.

3. HOW TO DEAL RUTHLESSLY WITH FAMILIAR SPIRITS.

4. OVERCOMING THE POWER OF WITCHCRAFT.

5. SOMETHING WORSE THAN WITCHCRAFT - AND ACIDIC PRAYERS TO OVERCOME IT.

6. FORTY TYPES OF PEOPLE YOU SHOULD NEVER HAND YOUR PULPIT TO.

7. FORTY REASONS WHY PEOPLE LEAVE YOUR CHURCH.

8. WHAT TO DO WHEN YOU THINK YOUR PASTOR IS WRONG.

9. 14 SURPRISING THINGS WE DO THAT PUT PEOPLE OFF CHRISTIANITY.

10. HIDDEN FACTS; ABOUT HOW JESUS CHRIST GREW HIS MINISTRY.

NOTES